BEING A
BETTER
PCC

HOW TO BE MORE EFFECTIVE IN THE LIFE
AND MISSION OF THE LOCAL CHURCH

John Cox

kevin
mayhew

First published in Great Britain in 2016 by Kevin Mayhew Ltd
Buxhall, Stowmarket, Suffolk IP14 3BW
Tel: +44 (0) 1449 737978 Fax: +44 (0) 1449 737834
E-mail: info@kevinmayhew.com

www.kevinmayhew.com

9 8 7 6 5 4 3 2 1 0

ISBN 978 1 84867 825 5
Catalogue No. 1501511

Cover design by Rob Mortonson
© Image used under licence from Shutterstock Inc.
Edited by Virginia Rounding
Typeset by Angela Selfe

Printed and bound in Great Britain

Contents

Acknowledgements

I am most grateful to James Hall, the Registrar in the diocese of St Edmundsbury and Ipswich, for his advice and corrections to the manuscript, eliminating my legal blunders.

PCCs and churchwardens should always take advice if they have any doubt about a matter of law. While I have tried to ensure that what is said in this book is legally correct, this is, as it says on the cover, only a brief guide and does not attempt to enter into the full complexities of the law which are necessarily subject to change over time.

About the author

Having spent rather a long time at various universities including Cambridge, Oxford and the University College of Rhodesia and Nyasaland, John was ordained to a curacy in the diocese of Liverpool in 1968. He spent a second curacy in an inner-city ex-slum parish in Birmingham and became rector in the same parish. After a five-year period at Church House, Westminster where he was Senior Selection Secretary, helping to select ordinands, he was made Canon Treasurer at Southwark Cathedral and Diocesan Director of Ordinands and Post-ordination training.

Following four years as Vicar of Roehampton he moved to become Archdeacon of Sudbury in the Diocese of St Edmundsbury and Ipswich in 1995. When he retired in 2006 he was asked to be the part-time Diocesan Director of Education, a job he did for nearly four and a half years before retiring for a second time. It has been during these retirement years that John has been writing for Kevin Mayhew, in between being chair of governors at a primary academy, playing golf and enjoying river cruises.

For details of all John Cox's books, please visit our website: www.kevinmayhew.com

Prologue

Geoff,

It was great to have a chat after church last week and I am glad you are willing to consider standing for the PCC.

I know you're away for a couple of weeks. Just a couple of points. We can talk further when you get back.

I could go on about it being a privilege to be on the PCC, a great opportunity to serve etc. And it is. But frankly we could do with your expertise. As you know, it's a small PCC and Brenda is our only churchwarden. She readily admits she knows nothing about buildings. We don't meet that often, but on the building side of things there is always something to do between meetings. So it will need some time given to it. If you agree to stand, I am sure everyone will be delighted and there will be no problem to get you elected - we're not that good at filling the vacancies we do have.

Of course you must not do it if you really don't want to – but I hope you will and that Sally will be happy about it as well.

Good luck with the conference etc.

Judy
The Revd Judy Cullip

Hi,

Thanks for the email. Just taking a break from a series of workshops.

I'll certainly think about it. I wouldn't be around all the time because of these business trips and you'll have to decide if that could be a problem. Obviously I know about buildings in general, but not much about medieval ones. Is there a tame architect we use?

I'm fairly new to the church so don't really know much about how PCCs work. Is there anything I could read up on it?

See you when I get back.

Geoff

Introduction

Geoff wouldn't be the first person to have their arm twisted to join a PCC – nor will he be the last. Experience varies enormously, of course, and there are still many churches where there is a contest to get on the PCC. Being a PCC member is seen not only as a privilege but also as a matter of status or even power. That is declining and, especially in rural communities and where church membership is small, getting people to stand for the PCC can be quite a struggle. To ensure that the PCC has members who actually have the skill and experience to enable it to carry out its responsibilities can be even harder. Care of the church fabric is only one such area.

Judy is wanting to be fair. She needs Geoff's expertise but she doesn't want to exert undue pressure. Certainly anything like emotional or religious blackmail would go against all she believes in. She needs Geoff to make an informed and realistic decision, aware of the commitment it may involve, given Geoff's business and family responsibilities, but not ignoring the fact that it is one way of serving the church.

Geoff has to give it careful thought. He doesn't want to say 'Yes' just to help Judy feel good and then never be available when he is needed. He wants to know more about what is involved and, being the sort of person he is, he'd like to know more about PCCs in general. He'd like to agree but he's not going to go into it with his eyes closed.

This brief guide to PCCs aims to help

- those who are considering standing,
- those who have only recently joined a PCC or never been really sure what is involved, and

- anyone who is just interested in what PCCs are for and what they get up to.

The list of contents could appear quite daunting, especially the number of PCC responsibilities. Don't be put off by that. Some knowledge is always helpful, but so is good common sense and for the more technical and legal matters there is always help available from diocesan officers. This guide is not meant to be exhaustive, nor does it constitute legal opinion and further reading and resources are suggested.

Believe it or not, PCCs can be fun and they certainly have a significant role to play – not always seen, not always appreciated, but real nevertheless. They are not simply administrative bodies dealing with church bureaucracy, but have an important role in the spiritual life and mission of the local church.

This is written from a Church of England standpoint. The 'constitution', membership and responsibilities of similar bodies in other churches and denominations will be somewhat different, reflecting their history, theology and ecclesiology.

Chapter 1

PCCs – what they are and where they came from

The parochial system

The parish and the parish council have secular origins in Anglo-Saxon times. The parish was a division of land with sufficient population and wealth to support a church and a priest, although it was only gradually that these were universally acquired. With the rise of the feudal system there was a reduction in the independence enjoyed by the *toun* (town) with its *moot* (meeting) to deal with local business. To rectify this, town councils were set up to deal with both civil and ecclesiastical matters. In rural areas the parish had originally equated to the manor, although this pattern became less clear as manors were divided through inheritance and population-distribution changed. It was normal for the priest, as the best-educated man locally, to chair the meeting, which was usually held in the church vestry. In time the feudal system decayed and these 'vestry meetings' gradually acquired greater powers, including the distribution of parish funds. By the Elizabethan era they had also become responsible for administering the support systems for the poor.

The Vestry

The parish vestry was thus in effect the parish church council, but with additional civic responsibilities. This situation continued until the nineteenth century, although the precise nature of the arrangements varied with the locality, especially in the urban areas. The parish records were secured in a parish chest for which the incumbent and churchwardens had keys, and it was the parish vestry that appointed officers such as churchwardens (as required by Canon Law), overseers of the poor, sextons and even night-watchmen. The primary responsibility of the 'vestry' was the care of the church and churchyard, but it was also variously responsible for common lands, roads and bridges, the parish workhouse, endowed charities and diverse other matters, such as weights and measures, stocks and whipping-posts, the destruction of vermin and keeping the peace. All this began to change in the nineteenth century as other organisations and boards took over many of these responsibilities. The Poor Law Amendment Act of 1834 meant that the relief of the poor was no longer the direct responsibility of the vestry. In 1894 elected parish councils and urban district councils were established under the Local Government Act, and all civic business was removed from the control of the vestry meeting.

The ecclesial responsibilities, including the administration and finance of the parish, were largely in the hands of the incumbent and the churchwardens, with the parishioners having little say apart from the election of the churchwardens. There was a growing desire among lay people to be more fully involved, as evidenced by the emergence of parochial church councils in some urban areas, although they existed and exercised powers at the discretion of the incumbent.

PCCs

PCCs were given legal status by the Church of England Assembly (Powers) Act of 1919 and the subsequent Parochial Church Councils (Powers) Measure of 1921 which defined their functions and powers. The further Measure of 1956 (as amended) is the current legal basis and defines the primary function of the PCC as:

co-operation with the minister in promoting in the parish the whole mission of the Church, pastoral, evangelistic, social and ecumenical.

We shall be looking more fully at the functions of the PCC in the next chapter.

In legal terms a PCC is a 'body corporate' – i.e., it is a legal entity regardless of the individuals who are its members for the time being and it exists for all time. ('Every council shall be a body corporate by the name of the parochial church council of the parish for which it is appointed and shall have perpetual succession.'[1])

PCCs are recognised as charitable bodies by the Charity Commission and, as such, it is important that the conduct of their affairs and the use of their assets are in accordance with the charitable purposes which the PCC is established to promote. PCC members are like any other charity trustees, with all the duties and responsibilities that role entails, and subject to general charity law as well as the specific requirements of Church of England law.

The Church Representation Rules, which were originally contained in Schedule 3 to the Synodical Government Measure 1969 (amended regularly over the years), constitute another important piece of legislation relevant to PCCs. As the name of the Measure indicates, it contains rules for how the governance of the Church of England is organised in its various bodies and the way their members are elected. It includes sections on General Synod, diocesan synods and deanery synods as well as PCCs. (See Chapter Four).

---

1. Parochial Church Council (Powers) Measure 1956, Section 3.

Chapter 2
PCCs – their powers and responsibilities

As we saw in the previous chapter, the old 'vestry meetings' had both civil and ecclesial powers. Under the Local Government Act of 1894, when rural and urban district councils and parish councils were set up, the vestries lost their civil responsibilities. The PCCs set up in 1921 retained the ecclesial powers, duties and liabilities of the vestry, apart from the election of churchwardens and sidesmen and the administration of ecclesiastical charities, most of which had already been transferred to other bodies or individuals. They gained the powers that churchwardens had previously held over the finances of the church and the care, maintenance and preservation of the fabric of the church and churchyard.

General powers

It is often incorrectly thought that PCCs are basically administrative bodies, simply keeping the parish church running. But, as the 1956 Measure indicates, their primary purpose is mission in all its forms. A PCC has the right to discuss any matter concerning the Church of England or any other matter of a religious or public interest. It can make recommendations to the deanery and diocesan synods and also inform them of the PCC's opinion on matters referred to it by the synods. There is thus a two-way relationship between the PCC and the synods.

Mission

It was Archbishop William Temple who reminded the Church that it exists for those who are not its members. It is God's partner and agent in his outgoing work of love for all. PCC agendas all too often give the lie to this, concentrating exclusively on 'churchy' matters and how to keep the organisation going. Administrative business does have to be dealt with, but everything should be done with the primary task of mission in mind.

Mission is a word bandied around a great deal in church circles these days, but without people necessarily understanding what it means. In 1986 the Anglican Consultative Council identified the following Five Marks of Mission:

- to proclaim the Good News of the Kingdom

- to teach, baptise and nurture new believers

- to respond to human need by loving service

- to seek to transform unjust structures of society, to challenge violence of every kind and pursue peace and reconciliation

- to strive to safeguard the integrity of creation, and sustain and renew the life of the earth.

No single one of the marks is mission. Mission is all of them together, although of course at different times and in different settings one or other may gain greater emphasis. Mission therefore embraces the evangelism and nurturing of individuals, loving service to all, issues of justice and peace and the care of the environment and created order. It should be top of a PCC's agenda.

Worship

What forms of services are used in a church is a matter of joint decision between the incumbent and the PCC. Legally, only those services that have been officially authorised under

Canon Law (Canons of the Church of England – Canon B1) should be used, but some flexibility is allowed, especially when it comes to all-age and non-eucharistic services. If the PCC and incumbent cannot agree, then the church must use the Book of Common Prayer services unless other authorised forms have been used regularly for at least two of the preceding four years. Where this is so, the PCC can insist that the alternative authorised services rather than the Book of Common Prayer services be used. The incumbent has the right to determine the forms of service for occasional offices (weddings, baptisms, funerals) (Canon B3).

The patterns of services, especially within a multi-parish benefice, can be complex and evoke strong feelings. An individual PCC may feel it is hard done by with only one service a month while the church near where the vicar lives gets four. Some common sense about the practicalities involved and some give-and-take should make it possible to arrive at an agreed pattern.

Worship is at the heart of a church's life – it is an encounter with God in which worshippers are 'formed and transformed'. It expresses what the church believes about God. Many people have their first experience of what the church is all about through attending an act of worship such as a baptism, wedding or funeral. It is therefore important that PCCs give time to review the worship, so that it not only meets the needs of current congregations, but is also accessible, meaningful and welcoming to enquirers and newcomers.

Buildings

Church buildings (especially those that are medieval and listed) can occupy a great deal of a PCC's time. Strictly, the church building 'belongs' to the incumbent. S/he holds the church keys. The churchwardens share 'possession' with the incumbent in that they each have rights of entry and the right to prevent people entering the church, but it is the PCC's responsibility to maintain and insure it. Buildings are both a delight and a headache. Their significance needs to be seen in the context of the visible presence of God in a community and as a physical resource in the church's mission. They are often also the bearers of hundreds of years of history and of a community's heritage. They witness to the faithfulness of countless worshippers and the commitment of those who have ensured that the building remains standing.

PCCs do not have the right to do what they like in a church and their role is that of stewards of the building. To ensure that whatever repairs, changes, reordering etc. it proposes are appropriate and in keeping, the PCC has to submit plans to the diocesan advisory committee (DAC) and obtain a faculty or other approval from the diocesan chancellor or archdeacon before any work can start (see Canon F13). A valuable resource to assist churchwardens and PCCs with the complications of the faculty process and maintenance matters in general is: *Caring for your Church Building* by James Halsall (Kevin Mayhew, 2015).

Church contents

The moveable furniture and artefacts of the church building are legally vested in the churchwardens. They are also subject to faculty jurisdiction, so permission will be required to remove any such objects, e.g., pews. The PCC is responsible for the insurance, care, maintenance and preservation of such goods and ornaments and it should provide a suitable safe for valuable articles and church documents. A record of alterations, additions, repairs and removals, whether to the building or its contents, must be kept in a suitable book.

Churchyard

Legal possession of the churchyard is jointly held by the churchwardens and the incumbent, but safety, maintenance, fencing and general care are the responsibility of the PCC. If the churchyard has been closed for future burials by an Order in Council, the PCC may by a formal notice pass its responsibilities to the appropriate local authority – e.g., a parish council. In such a case, the precise extent of the local authority's duties is not entirely clear, and the PCC should continue to be alert to potential hazards and liaise with the local authority if headstones etc. are no longer safe (see below). All churchyards (open or closed) are subject to faculty jurisdiction.

A PCC should include the churchyard in its public liability insurance.

Only residents of the parish or people on the church electoral roll at the time of their death have a right to be buried in the churchyard (assuming it is still open), but not in any particular spot. A PCC may agree to someone being allowed to **reserve a grave space**. This must be minuted at a PCC meeting and the person or their representative(s) should then make a faculty application to the diocesan registrar. Normally the person reserving a space should be at least middle-aged and have a close connection with the parish. Any grant of a faculty will usually require a fee to be paid to the PCC as a contribution towards the maintenance of the churchyard.

The diocese will have churchyard rules as to what **memorial stones** an incumbent may allow. These can be obtained from the diocesan advisory committee (DAC) and, if the incumbent and family cannot agree something within the rules, the family must apply for a faculty. Where there are old headstones and families are no longer able to care for the graves (simply because there are no family members left or they have all moved to other parts of the country) it is the responsibility of the PCC to ensure that headstones and vault memorials are safe. Any repair will normally need a faculty.

Any changes in the **general appearance** of the churchyard that a PCC proposes, such as the erection of a toilet or major work on trees, will need planning permission as well as a faculty. Trees may be protected by tree preservation orders or fall within a conservation area, in which case the PCC will need the permission of the local authority to lop or fell them. Doing so without permission constitutes a criminal offence and substantial fines can be imposed. Notice-boards will also need a faculty or similar consent and, depending on size, planning permission may also be required.

Cremation is increasingly common and some people like to place **cremated remains** in a churchyard. A PCC may set aside an area for this in the churchyard. Consideration should be given to the size of the plaques to ensure the space is not filled too quickly and questions of maintenance should also be discussed – e.g., mowing the area. Will vases be allowed on or by the plaques? To assist with maintenance some PCCs prefer to have a single 'wall' created to which individual plaques can be fixed or to use an existing wall. An alternative to plaques is the provision of a book of remembrance in the church. All of these possibilities will require faculty permission.

Finances

New or prospective PCC members are sometimes anxious that they will be personally responsible for any liabilities of the PCC. This is not the case since the PCC is a separate legal entity, separate from the individual members who make it up. So a contract entered into by a PCC continues even if the individual members of the PCC change. Any liabilities of the PCC do not fall on its individual members, unless they have been dishonest or obviously reckless.

The PCC is a charity and PCC members are charity trustees. As such they are responsible for ensuring that the PCC's financial arrangements, management and reporting are in accordance with the relevant laws and regulations. The Charity Commission publishes extensive guidance, which is kept up to date as the Charities Acts (the current one is 2011) and the SORPs (which set out accounting requirements) change. PCCs are currently not required to register with the Charity Commission or file annual returns unless their annual income exceeds £100,000, but they must prepare their annual reports and financial statements in accordance with the requirements of the Charities Act 2011 and make them available to the public.

As a charity the PCC needs to be aware that the money at its disposal must be used for its charitable purposes – i.e., 'promoting in the parish the whole mission of the Church, pastoral, evangelistic, social and ecumenical'.[2] Care has to be taken when it comes to donating to another charity. The charity receiving the donation must be involved with activities that assist or further the work of the PCC. There should be no conflict of interests, so a member of the PCC

---

2. Parochial Church Council (Powers) Measure 1956, Section 2, 2(a).

should not benefit personally from the donation, and the donation should not put the PCC's financial viability at risk. If in doubt, take advice.

The PCC should appoint a treasurer from among its membership. If a treasurer is not appointed, the role must be undertaken by a churchwarden or another suitable person, who does not thereby become a member of the PCC unless co-opted.

The PCC's gross income will determine how the accounts are prepared and whether they require an annual inspection by an independent examiner or a full audit.

For further information and details, reference should be made to www.parishresources.org.uk – the Parish Finance section.

Appointments

Employment law is highly complex and, unless specialist knowledge is available through one of its members, a PCC would be wise to take advice when entering into any form of employment contract. Only the most basic information is provided here.

PCCs do not legally employ their ministers but they may well recruit to other posts, full-time or part-time. These could include administrator, organist, cleaners, verger, gardener, youth worker. Such people may well be treated as employees of the PCC for legal purposes and specialist advice may be necessary, as there are numerous legal and tax requirements on employers. Whatever their status, the PCC must also comply with equal opportunities and safeguarding legislation.

The Equality Act 2010 seeks to protect people against discrimination, harassment or victimisation in connection with their work. The characteristics protected under the legislation are:

- age
- disability
- gender reassignment
- race
- religion or belief
- sex
- sexual orientation
- marriage and civil partnership
- pregnancy and maternity.

Organised religious bodies are allowed some exceptions so that appointments do not conflict with their doctrinal beliefs, but they must be applied very carefully.

Appointments where the person will be in regular and/or unsupervised contact with children or vulnerable adults are subject to Disclosure and Barring Service (DBS) checks. See page 32 under 'Safeguarding'.

PCCs should ensure that they are 'good employers' and this means they should give serious consideration to paying and treating their employees more generously than the minimum standards set by the law.

Data protection

When the 1998 Data Protection Act (DPA) was introduced many parishes thought it did not relate to them because they did not keep vast details of personal information nor share them with other organisations. This was a mistaken view.

All parishes collect and keep personal information. One has only to think of the church electoral roll, names and addresses of congregation members, information about baptisms, weddings and funerals, information collected in the course of fund-raising and organising social events, and pastoral contacts. As soon as something is done with that personal information (e.g., the vicar passes a name and address to the PCC secretary to create a contact list), it is deemed to have been processed and that means it comes under the scope of the Act.

For purposes of the Act every PCC and incumbent is regarded as a *data controller* – i.e., they determine the purpose for which data is processed and the manner in which this is done. However, the majority of PCCs will be able to claim exemption from having to notify the Information Commissioner's Office, provided that the data is held and used only in normal church administration. Incumbents will need to notify if they keep records of pastoral care discussions on computer, assuming such records concern beliefs, relationships and opinions, rather than purely factual information such as dates of birth or baptism. Details can be seen on the following website: www.ico.org.uk.

Special care is needed in the keeping and processing of what is deemed 'sensitive personal data'. This includes data that relates to an individual's racial or ethnic origin, their religious beliefs and political opinions, physical and mental health condition, sexual life, and alleged or actual criminal activity and record. Keeping a record of such information in a paper filing cabinet in such a way that it could be readily accessed – e.g., with files in alphabetical order – is covered by the Act as well as keeping information on a computer.

Eight principles set out in Schedule 1 of the DPA must be observed in storing and processing personal data. Inter alia, PCCs must obtain a person's permission to hold and use their personal information; only relevant information should be kept and not for longer than is necessary; it should be kept secure and up to date.

PCCs should note that an individual has the right, within certain limits, to request access to the information being kept about them. The PCC may charge for this but must provide the information within 40 days. If providing such information would also mean that another individual's personal details will be disclosed then, unless that person gives permission, the PCC does not have to provide the information. PCCs are not subject to Freedom of Information legislation.

In the above I have provided very general information and more information can be found at the following links:

www.ico.org.uk

www.lambethpalacelibrary.org/files/data_protection_final.pdf.

Disability Discrimination

Few people would disagree that churches should be places of welcome – in their approach to mission, pastoral care, worship and in their buildings – and it is part of the PCC's responsibility to see that this is a reality and not just a pious hope. Ensuring that what the church offers is physically, mentally and spiritually accessible to all involves a sensitive approach to those who have a long-term physical or mental disability. The obligation for the church to be accessible to all is founded in the gospel and in God's mission to everyone and thus goes well beyond the law, but there is also a legal requirement under the Disability Discrimination Acts of 1995 and 2005.

To get a sense of what this may entail, PCC members could try the following:

- Visit their church in a wheelchair or blindfolded

- Try to follow a service without access to any printed material (e.g., service books, hymn books, notice sheets) or without being able to hear what is happening.

The Act requires the PCC to make reasonable adjustments, but these will depend on individual circumstances. While accessibility means much more than just getting into and around a building, this often provides a particular headache to PCCs, especially if the church is historic, medieval and listed. Steps up or down into church may be a hazard not only for wheelchairs but also for people with gammy legs. A ramp may be the answer but should this be permanent or temporary? Will it meet faculty requirements? The size of space immediately beyond the steps may make it difficult to provide a ramp that meets health and safety requirements. Steps up to the chancel and altar rail are an additional problem and a rail may not always be possible. If the physical barrier cannot be overcome then, for example, a choir member may need to process to their stall a different way and the priest may have to administer communion to someone in the pew.

> This is an example of a change in practice which would be seen as a reasonable adjustment to meet the needs of the individual, but in other cases it may be reasonable for the PCC to buy or install something. The provision of a 'hearing loop' in the sound system or large-print hymn and service books may be needed.

More difficult is the provision of toilet facilities – relevant here, as well as generally, since 'continence' is one of the 'categories' included under the test for what constitutes a disability.

The Act does use the word 'reasonable' and a PCC should consult the DAC for help in meeting the needs of equal access. Its financial resources will be relevant.

A helpful online document can be found at:

https://www.churchofengland.org/media/49533/advisory notefive.pdf.

Fire prevention

A major church fire is devastating for the congregation and for the community even when there is no loss of life or injury. Mitigating the risk of fire is part of the PCC's general responsibility for the care of the church building.

Under the Regulatory Reform (Fire Safety) Order 2005 the PCC is required to appoint a 'responsible person' who should carry out a comprehensive fire-risk assessment (or ensure that it is done). In many churches this will be a churchwarden or the PCC's building officer. Where the church has employees, it is the PCC itself who is the 'responsible person'. The assessment should be undertaken regularly. A suitable form for this can be found at the following link:

http://www.ecclesiastical.com/ChurchMatters/Images/fire-risk-assessment-form.pdf.

The PCC will need:

- to provide suitable fire extinguishers (at least two) and churchwardens and sidespeople should know where they are and how to use them

- to deal with any dangerous substances discovered through the assessment

- to set in place procedures for managing risks – e.g., to ensure candles are used safely

- to undertake regular electricity and lighting inspections
- to ensure appropriate signage is in place
- to ensure that any employees are aware of fire-safety procedures
- to ensure that when the building is in use, exit doors are unlocked.

Where the PCC has responsibility for buildings other than the church, risk assessments will also need to be made for each of them, together with appropriate arrangements if they are used by other groups or organisations.

Useful websites:

http://www.ecclesiastical.com/churchmatters/churchguidance/fireguidance/index.aspx

http://www.london.anglican.org/kb/fire-safety-in-churches/

and other diocesan sites.

In addition, very detailed information can be found at:

https://www.gov.uk/government/publications/fire-safety-risk-assessment-small-and-medium-places-of-assembly.

Health and Safety

There are plenty of jokes and myths about health and safety, but not when someone is injured because proper safety measures were not in place or when a PCC is fined or sued. PCCs are responsible for ensuring that their church employees (and this includes volunteers), congregations and visitors are safe –

in church, in churchyards, in church halls and any other premises that the church owns or occupies. The responsibilities are covered by the Health and Safety at Work etc. Act 1974 and numerous regulations.

A PCC needs to know what its risks are and therefore the first thing is to ensure that a health and safety risk assessment has been made *and is kept up to date*. A form for this can be found at the following very useful website, which provides a wide range of relevant guidance notes and advice:

http://www.ecclesiastical.com/churchmatters/churchguidance/ churchhealthandsafety/index.aspx.

The types of risk are considerable and run from trip hazards to dangerous electrical installations, from flammable liquids to weedkiller. **Ladders** are a particular hazard, falls from ladders being the cause of 20% of all workplace fatalities. The 68-year-old churchwarden may have been climbing ladders all his life, but that does not mean he is safe. There are clear guidelines about securing ladders, training and supervision. It may feel 'over the top' but it is better than risking an accident.

If a PCC employs **contractors** for such purposes as building or maintenance works, tree surgery or window cleaning, it is important that it not only checks their insurance cover but also their health and safety procedures and their professional qualifications. For major building works the Construction (Design and Management) Regulations may apply and the PCC should take advice from its architect or surveyor on what this entails.

Asbestos is a particular hazard and if a PCC thinks it may be in any of its buildings, it must commission a suitable and sufficient survey to establish if there is indeed asbestos and, if so, its type, quantity and condition. A plan should then be produced indicating the risk, and how the PCC will manage it. Anyone who is liable to work in the vicinity of the asbestos must be informed.

Bells should not be left in the 'up' position. If circumstances do require it, then there should be clear procedures in place to manage the risk – e.g., warning notices, access doors locked and the keys secure.

Every church is different and undertakes different activities. It is therefore vital that the PCC takes health and safety seriously and interprets any general advice in the light of local circumstances. If there is an accident then it should be recorded and where it results in serious injury this must be reported to the responsible authority (normally the local authority) – see the Reporting of Injuries, Diseases and Dangerous Occurrences Regulations 2013 (available at http://www.hse.gov.uk/riddor/).

It is vital that the PCC ensures that they have appropriate and adequate insurance.

Safeguarding

The abuse of children and young people has made horrendous headlines in recent years. Celebrities have been imprisoned, and people in high places have been under scrutiny. Churches that had been thought to be above such things have been found to be sadly wanting and the scandals in Ireland and elsewhere have sent shock waves through the Roman Catholic Church and others. The high reputation churches have had for care and trust has been tainted. And it was, in part, that very reputation for trust that made the churches vulnerable – to the predatory paedophile and to the cover up of abuse. 'It couldn't happen here' is sadly still sometimes heard in church circles.

There are those who work with youngsters in Sunday schools or youth groups who still complain bitterly that they are not being trusted when they are asked to complete the necessary checks. The reasons for such checks are in fact all too obvious and the law requires them.

The enquiry into the infamous case of Victoria Climbié (2003) resulted in new legislation with the Children Act of 2004 and widened the scope of 'child protection' to the 'safeguarding of children'.

Safeguarding of children has been defined as:

The process of protecting children from abuse or neglect, preventing impairment of their health and development, and ensuring they are growing up in circumstances consistent with the provision of safe and effective care that enables children to have optimum life chances and enter adulthood successfully. (Ofsted)

Safeguarding also extends to vulnerable adults.

PCCs have the responsibility to adopt and implement a safeguarding policy and procedures and, with the incumbent, to appoint a parish safeguarding officer. The officer should be a member of the PCC or at least attend meetings, will require an enhanced Disclosure and Barring Service (DBS) check and should have undergone appropriate training. The role includes:

- reviewing the policy and procedures

- ensuring that any safeguarding concerns are properly and promptly communicated to the appropriate authorities

- ensuring the safe recruitment both of paid staff and volunteers

- ensuring that parental consents and emergency contact details are kept for each child.

Every diocese will have detailed guidelines and pro-formae available to assist the safeguarding officer and the PCC to fulfil their responsibilities.

Useful websites:

https://www.churchofengland.org/clergy-office-holders/protecting-and-safeguarding-children-and-vulnerable-adults.aspx.

https://www.gov.uk/government/publications/safeguarding-children-and-young-people/safeguarding-children-and-young-people

The press

While a PCC may be delighted if the annual fête or a special Christmas concert receives a favourable mention in the local newspaper, there tends to be a cautious attitude towards the press in general, especially when it is the newspaper that makes the first move. Editors like stories that will sell papers so a hint of disagreement among a congregation or between the vicar and the PCC will get a reporter excited. The sniff of an even greater scandal may get the nationals on the phone or, worse still, on the doorstep.

It is right to be cautious. There are issues of privacy, confidentiality and even of legal process that may be involved. Unless there is someone on the PCC who has experience and skill in dealing with the media, it is generally wise to contact the diocesan communications officer before saying anything. A polite refusal to give an initial comment but with a promise to get back to the reporter is a good tactic and usually well understood by the reporter. Don't be bullied.

Sometimes the press asks to see PCC minutes. It is perfectly reasonable to enquire why they are wanted and for what purpose. You may not always get a straight answer! As a general rule, minutes should not be made available to anyone outside the PCC until they have been agreed and signed. The PCC may decide that any minutes (or part of them) must remain confidential and it is best to do this at the meeting concerned. Where the PCC has not made such a decision and the minutes have been agreed and signed, the press has no right to see them, but members of the church electoral roll do and are free to disclose them, so it will be difficult for the PCC to deny the press access. If in doubt contact the diocesan registrar or diocesan communications officer.

Vacancies

While it is normal for the incumbent to be the chair of the PCC, in their absence or during a vacancy (interregnum) the elected lay vice-chair takes on this role.

Vacancies can be a time of considerable anxiety for a PCC but, in some cases, they may actually offer a time of development and growth in lay confidence. It will of course depend on the past relationship between the PCC and the incumbent and how long the vacancy lasts. It is the churchwardens who bear the major responsibility, usually assisted by the rural or area dean.

Increasingly, patrons and bishops seek to involve the parish as much as possible in the appointment process, including at the interview. Patrons have historical rights to 'present' a candidate, but normally, when pastoral re-organisation is likely, the patron's rights will be suspended and the process will be more in the hands of the bishop or archdeacon.

When a vacancy has been announced, the PCC will be asked to appoint two representatives. These need not necessarily be the churchwardens, but people whom the PCC considers to be best suited to represent the needs of the parish in the selection and interviewing of candidates. Ultimately they will give or withhold their approval to the patron's or bishop's choice.

The archdeacon will usually meet the PCC to discuss the parish's needs and the PCC will be asked to draw up a parish profile and decide whether or not to ask the bishop or patron(s) to advertise the post. Some patrons insist on seeing only one candidate at a time and do not advertise, although this is increasingly rare. The patron and bishop may also write a statement concerning the parish within the wider diocesan context. The PCC may request a meeting with the bishop and patron(s) to discuss their views and the process of appointment.

The PCC should decide whether or not it wishes to pass or review a resolution about the acceptability of women as priests in the parish and whether or not it seeks to set any other job requirements within those allowed by equal opportunities legislation.

The PCC should then prepare an information pack and, if more than one candidate has applied, a shortlist will need to be produced and references taken up. The PCC representatives will then normally attend the interviews and, after the bishop has seen the recommended candidate, an announcement can be made.

Circumstances and local diocesan practice will mean that the details of this process will vary.

The PCC should hold the whole process in its prayers.

A useful website is:

https://www.churchofengland.org/media/1291742/towards%20good%20practice%20for%20the%20web.htm.

Chapter 3

Annual Church Meetings

The Annual Meeting of Parishioners to appoint Churchwardens

Churchwardens are officers of the bishop, not of the incumbent nor of the PCC. The appointment is made annually at a meeting of parishioners. Under the Churchwardens Measure 2001 this meeting is required to take place before 30 April. Originally the requirement was 'not later in the year than during the week following Easter week', hence the popular name for the meeting: 'The Easter Vestry Meeting'. People whose names are on the church electoral roll of the parish and those who are resident in the parish and have their names on the register of local government electors may attend. The latter do not have to be members of the Church of England.

Tenure

Churchwardens hold office for a year at a time and, to encourage the involvement of more laity in positions of responsibility, the Measure makes the general rule that the maximum continuous period of service should be six years and that subsequent reappointment should only occur after a break of two years. A meeting of parishioners may pass a resolution that this norm does not apply in their parish, but careful thought should be exercised before doing so. The decision can be revoked at a subsequent meeting of parishioners.

BEING A BETTER PCC

Eligibility

To be eligible for appointment as churchwarden a person must be baptised, and the bishop has no power to dispense with this requirement. In addition:

a. The person's name must be on the electoral roll of the parish (without this the churchwarden could not be a member of the PCC).

b. The person must be 'an actual communicant', meaning that the person must have received communion at least three times in the previous twelve months, and either be confirmed or desirous of confirmation or a baptised communicant in good standing in another church that subscribes to the doctrine of the Trinity.

c. The person must be over 21 years of age.

Under exceptional circumstances, a bishop may dispense with any or all of these latter three requirements, but parishes must convince the bishop of the need to do so.

The parish priest's spouse may be appointed a churchwarden, but only after careful consideration.

Consent

The elected churchwarden must have signified on the nomination form that he/she is willing to stand. A person may only serve as churchwarden in more than one parish simultaneously where the parishes are in the same multi-parish benefice, or in benefices held in plurality (i.e., having the same incumbent) or looked after by the same minister.

Disqualification

There are a number of reasons why a person could be disqualified from being a churchwarden:

- They are disqualified from being a charity trustee under charity legislation.

- They have a conviction for a criminal offence under Schedule 1 to the Children and Young Persons Act 1933.

- If the bishop has disqualified the person in the case of a breakdown in the pastoral relationship between the incumbent and parishioners under the Incumbents (Vacation of Benefices) Measure 1977.

Election

The meeting of parishioners is convened by a notice signed by the minister, indicating the date, time and place of the meeting. This notice should be fixed to or near to the main door of the parish church (and all other buildings licensed for public worship in the parish) for a period including the last two Sundays before the meeting. It is important that the notice is placed so that it is easy for non-churchgoers to see it.

Two people, who are eligible to attend the meeting (not the minister), need to nominate and second each candidate in writing and the paper should also have a statement signed by the nominated person that they are willing to stand and are not disqualified (see above). Nomination forms should reach the minister before the meeting starts and should be retained for at least one year after the election. It is desirable that the incumbent and laity should agree on the suitability of a candidate.

Procedure

a. The meeting is normally chaired by the minister. Where a minister is not present, the meeting chooses the chair.

b. If the number of candidates is equal to or less than the number of places to be filled, all the candidates are declared elected. (Most parishes have two churchwardens but for historic reasons some parishes have more.)

c. If there are more candidates than vacancies to be filled, an election takes place either by paper vote (the paper being signed on the reverse side by the voter) or, if agreed by the meeting, by a show of hands.

d. Anyone eligible to attend the meeting has the right to vote, apart from the minister.

e. A voter cannot give more than one vote to each candidate but has as many votes as there are places to be filled.

f. If candidates receive equal votes, the decision is made by lot.

g. The result of the election should be announced as soon as possible and a notice with the result posted on or near the main church door of all places licensed for public worship in the parish for at least 14 days.

If a minister believes that the election of a particular person as churchwarden would result in serious difficulties of trust and relationships, it is possible for the minister to tell the meeting prior to the election that only one churchwarden will be elected by those present. The minister then chooses one of those nominated, the result is announced and the election of the other churchwarden then follows. Such action is exceptional and the minister has no right of veto.

Casual vacancy

Occasionally casual vacancies will occur among the elected lay members of the PCC or the deanery synod. They also arise when insufficient candidates have been nominated to fill all the available places at the annual meeting. Where the annual parochial church meeting is not due within the next two months, the PCC itself may – and, in the case of a deanery synod representative, must – elect a qualified person to fill the vacant place. In the case of the deanery synod, the name of the person filling the vacancy should be sent to the deanery synod secretary and the diocesan electoral registration officer.

Admission

Churchwardens do not take up their office until they have been admitted by the bishop or his substitute (usually an archdeacon). This is normally as part of an act of worship and must take place prior to 31 July. If this does not happen, a casual vacancy occurs. A churchwarden who has been re-elected must still be admitted in the year of re-election.

Duties

Churchwardens have the responsibility of representing the laity and co-operating with the incumbent.

  a. They are to encourage the laity in their faith ('the practice of true religion'[3]), to promote unity and peace and to ensure there is 'order and decency in the church and churchyard, especially during times of divine service'.[4] This includes the right to direct people where to sit (or not sit) in the church.

  b. They have the care of 'plate, ornaments and the moveable goods of the church'.[5] They are required to keep and

---

3. Canons of the Church of England, Canon E 1.4.
4. Ibid.
5. Canon E 1.5

revise as necessary an inventory of these objects and a record (terrier) of any land owned by the parish.

c. They are to keep a log book in which any alterations, additions or repairs made to the church building are recorded. The log should also record the location of documents relating to such alterations, additions and repairs.

d. They should carry out an annual inspection of the church fabric and contents and make an annual report to the Annual Parochial Church Meeting (APCM) on these.

e. They should report annually on the state of the parish through the questions asked in the archdeacon's articles of enquiry.

f. They are members of the PCC, subject to normal eligibility.

g. They fulfil the role of treasurer if the PCC, for whatever reason, fails to appoint one.

h. They may, by virtue of their office, be trustees of parochial charities.

i. They act as sequestrators during a vacancy together with any appointed by the bishop, such as the rural dean. On behalf of the bishop they ensure continuity of church services, pastoral oversight within the parish and care of the parsonage house.

Deputy and assistant churchwardens

Deputy churchwardens have a legal status under the Church Representation Rules but are not the bishop's officers and exercise their functions as delegated to them by the churchwardens. They are elected annually. Assistant churchwardens have no legal status and are chosen to assist the churchwardens as directed by them. Neither is obligatory and parishes may decide to have them for a variety of reasons, but usually to ensure continuity and succession and to share responsibilities.

The Annual Parochial Church Meeting (APCM)

The APCM must be held before 30 April and very often follows immediately after the annual meeting of parishioners. To be able to attend, lay people must have their names on the church electoral roll. The incumbent or priest-in-charge and the following other clergy may attend:

a. those licensed to the parish

b. those resident in the parish and not beneficed or licensed to another parish

c. those declared by the PCC to be habitual worshippers in the parish

d. those who are co-opted members of the PCC

e. those who are members of the team ministry (if applicable)

f. incumbents and priests-in-charge of a group ministry of which the parish is a member.

The Electoral Roll

Every parish is required to have a church electoral roll. Lay persons may have their name entered on the roll if:

a. they are baptised

b. they are 16 years old or above

   c. they sign an application form for enrolment and in it declare that they are:

     1. a member of the Church of England (or Church in communion with it) and resident in the parish, or

     2. a member of the Church of England (or Church in communion) and have regularly worshipped in the parish during the previous six months, or

     3. a member of another Church that subscribes to the doctrine of the Holy Trinity, and wish to be a member of the Church of England and have worshipped regularly in the parish during the previous six months.

A person may be on the electoral roll of more than one parish, but must choose only one to represent on the deanery synod.

A person's name shall be removed from the electoral roll if they:

   a. have died

   b. been ordained

   c. express the wish in writing to have their name removed

   d. no longer live in the parish, unless they continue to worship regularly in it (unless prevented by illness or other sufficient cause)

   e. do not live in the parish and have not worshipped regularly in it during the previous six months (unless prevented by illness or other sufficient cause).

The PCC has to appoint an electoral roll officer and it is their task to revise the roll each year. Notice of the revision should be fixed to or near the main door of the parish church and all other buildings licensed for public worship 14 days before the revision. The revision should be completed not more than 28 and not less than 15 days before the APCM. The revised roll together with a list of those names removed since the last revision must be published and placed near the main door of the parish church for at least 14 days before the APCM so that errors and omissions can be corrected. The electoral roll officer or other PCC officer should inform the secretary of the diocesan synod of the number of names on the roll by 1 June after each APCM.

A completely new roll has to be prepared every six years (2019, 2026 etc.) and notice of this given two months prior to the APCM of that year. It should be published 14 days before the APCM, giving people the opportunity to correct errors or omissions.

Convening

A notice convening the APCM has to be fixed on or near to the main door of the parish church and any other building in the parish licensed for public worship, for a period including the last two Sundays prior to the meeting. The date, time and place of the meeting will be in accordance with the direction of the previous APCM or of the PCC (which can overrule the APCM) or, if there was no such direction, by the decision of the minister.

Procedure

a. The meeting is normally chaired by the minister or, in the minister's absence, by the vice-chair.

b. The chair has a deciding vote except in the case of elections.

c. Anyone with the right to attend may ask questions or raise a relevant matter for discussion.

d. The PCC secretary (or other person appointed by the meeting) shall record the minutes of the meeting.

Business
will include:

a. The report of the electoral roll officer of any changes in the roll.

b. An annual report on the work of the PCC and activities of the parish in general.

c. The audited or examined financial statement of the PCC for the year ending the previous 31 December.

d. A report on the fabric, goods and ornaments of the church.

e. A report on the proceedings of the deanery synod.

f. The election of lay representatives to the deanery synod (every three years).

g. The election of lay representatives to the PCC.

h. The appointment of sidespeople.

i. The appointment of an auditor or independent examiner.

Some parishes have a 'composite' annual report prepared prior to the meeting incorporating items a to e and allow time for questions on any part of it. This can give them time to consider wider issues, such as the mission strategy of the parish.

Election of PCC members and Deanery Synod representatives
Lay PCC members must be elected annually at the APCM and lay representatives of the PCC on the deanery synod every three years.

a. Lay people are eligible for election if:

   1. their name has been on the electoral roll for at least six months

   2. they are 16 years old or above

   3. they are an 'actual communicant'

   4. they have indicated their willingness to serve.

b. All candidates must be nominated and seconded by persons eligible to attend the APCM either prior to or at the meeting.

c. If the number of candidates does not exceed the number of vacancies they are declared elected; otherwise, an election takes place at the meeting.

d. No ordained person is allowed to vote in the election of parochial representatives of the laity.

e. Those voting have as many votes as there are candidates but must not give a candidate more than one vote.

f. Voting can be by a show of hands unless someone objects and then it is a paper vote, with the voter signing the reverse of the paper.

g. If an election results in an equal number of votes, the decision is made by lot.

h. The result of the election should be announced as soon as possible and a notice with the result posted on or near the main church door of all places licensed for public worship in the parish for at least 14 days.

i. The PCC secretary should send the names and addresses of the elected lay deanery synod representatives to the diocesan electoral registration officer.

The procedures and requirements that have been set out in this chapter apply directly to single parish benefices. In teams, groups, united parishes and multi-parish benefices there are minor differences and these can be checked in the relevant regulations:

The Churchwardens Measure 2001

The Church Representation Rules 2011 © The Archbishops' Council

These can both be viewed on line:

https://www.churchofengland.org/about-us/structure/churchlawlegis/legislation/measures.aspx

https://www.churchofengland.org/about-us/structure/churchlawlegis/church-representation-rules/church-representation-rules-online.aspx.

Chapter 4

PCC Membership

Members

The membership of a PCC consists of members by virtue of their office (ex officio), those elected at the APCM (see page 46) and co-opted members.

The ex officio members are:

- all priests and deacons licensed to the parish

- deaconesses and licensed lay workers licensed to the parish

- other clergy in the ministry team (where the parish is in a team ministry)

- such readers licensed to the parish and on the electoral roll as have been decided by the APCM

- the churchwardens (so long as they are 'actual communicants' and on the electoral roll)

- any person on the electoral roll who is a member of a deanery, diocesan or General Synod.

The house of laity of a deanery synod elects lay representatives to the diocesan synod and General Synod.

A person ceases to be a member of the PCC:

- if their name is removed from the electoral roll

- if they refuse to have their name put on a new electoral roll when it is revised

- if they are disqualified from being a charity trustee

- if they are disqualified by the decision of the bishop

- in the case of elected and co-opted members, when their term of office ends (see below)

- in the case of ex officio members, when they cease to hold the office.

Numbers

The number of elected lay representatives on a PCC is determined by the number of names on the electoral roll.

- 6 lay elected members where there are not more than 50 on the roll

- 9 lay elected members where there are not more than 100 on the roll

- 12 lay elected members where there are not more than 200 on the roll

- 15 lay elected members where there are more than 200 on the roll.

The APCM may alter these numbers, but the alteration cannot take effect until the next APCM.

Co-option

The PCC is able to co-opt additional members at any time during the year and they serve until the end of the next APCM. There should not be more co-opted members than make up one fifth of the number of lay representatives, or two, whichever is the greater. Co-opted members may be clergy or lay. The reasons for co-option will vary, but sometimes this is the only way to fill a particular post – e.g., a secretary or treasurer.

Term of office

The normal rule is that elected lay PCC members hold office for three years, with one third (those who have served longest) retiring and being eligible for re-election at the APCM each year. The APCM may nevertheless decide that all must retire annually but not so as to affect any existing terms of office of those already in post. Such a decision must be reviewed at least once every six years. Members elected during the year to fill a casual vacancy serve until the end of the term they fill. Those who are members of a PCC by virtue of being elected as lay members of a deanery synod continue to be PCC members until 31 May following the election of their successors.

Officers

Chair

The incumbent or minister of the parish is the chair of the PCC, and the PCC elects a lay person as vice-chair. The minister may of course ask the vice-chair to take the chair for certain meetings or parts of meetings. This may be particularly appropriate if a subject having direct relevance to the minister is being discussed or where the minister wishes to make a particular contribution. During a prolonged absence of the minister or during a vacancy the vice-chair acts as, and has the full powers vested in, the chair. The chair will normally draw up the agenda for PCC meetings, often in consultation with the secretary, and is responsible for managing the meeting.

Secretary

The PCC will normally elect one of its members to act as secretary. When this is not possible, a suitable person who is not a member must be appointed to undertake the role.

If eligible, they may then be co-opted on to the PCC, but this is not obligatory and the PCC may already have its full quota of co-opted members. If the secretary is not a member of the PCC, the PCC may offer appropriate remuneration.

The secretary

- is responsible for and has charge of the documents that relate to the business of the PCC. This does not include the electoral roll unless the secretary is also the electoral roll officer;

- keeps the minutes and records any resolutions passed by the PCC;

- informs the diocesan and deanery secretary of their name and address and is the normal contact person between the PCC and the deanery and diocese;

- deals with any correspondence relating to the PCC;

- helps to ensure the smooth running of the PCC by careful preparation and distribution of relevant papers.

Treasurer

The PCC will normally elect one or more of its members to act as treasurer. When no one is available among the PCC membership, the PCC can appoint a suitable person who is not a member in the same way as for the secretary and the same comments apply. If all else fails, a churchwarden must act as treasurer.

The treasurer

- is responsible for the management of the financial affairs of the PCC, and for recording and checking any financial transactions carried out on behalf of the PCC;

- acts at the direction of the PCC;

- monitors the accounts and ensures financial obligations are met;

- drafts an annual budget;

- prepares the accounts and financial statements for the auditor or independent examiner and for presentation to the APCM.

Electoral roll officer

The electoral roll officer is normally elected from among the PCC members, but a person who is not a member may also be appointed. This position is sometimes also held by the PCC secretary. It is the responsibility of the electoral roll officer to keep the electoral roll, to revise it and to create a new roll at the appropriate time. (For further details see The Electoral Roll in Chapter Three).

Sidespeople

Sidespeople are normally appointed at the APCM but if the need arises the appointment can be made by the PCC. Anyone whose name is on the church electoral roll is eligible. Canon E 2.3 states that their duty is 'to promote the cause of true religion in the parish and to assist the churchwardens in the discharge of their duties in maintaining order and decency in the church and churchyard, especially during the time of divine service'. In practice most sidespeople ensure that people are welcomed into church at a service, distribute service and hymn books and take the collection.

In addition to members of the PCC, many people assist the PCC and minister in the running and work of the church. Among them will be choirs, church cleaners, welcomers, flower arrangers, those who provide refreshments, magazine contributors and editors, those who help tidy the churchyard, Sunday school leaders, pastoral carers and a whole host of others. Some have very specific roles carried out by paid employees or volunteers.

Verger

In cathedrals and many large churches the verger(s) will be paid employees of the PCC, but for most churches the role of verger is likely to be carried out by a volunteer. The name 'verger' or 'virger' comes from the rod or staff they carry at the head of a ceremonial procession or to precede readers or preachers to the lectern or pulpit, and which were sometimes used to keep order. Although the need to control congregations in this way is seldom necessary these days, the role continues. Vergers are recorded as being on the staff of cathedrals as early as the twelfth century.

Good vergers are those who are not really noticed, going about their duties quietly and without drawing attention to themselves. They are usually recognised by their black gown, on the sleeve of which there may be the badge of the Guild of Vergers which depicts crossed verger's rods.

The other duties of vergers vary enormously, depending upon the needs of the church, but they may include:

- opening up and locking of the church
- preparing the church for worship, including the care of altar linen and altar frontals
- ensuring the supply of wine and wafers for Holy Communion, and other requirements such as candles
- setting out vestments

- general 'housekeeping'
- checking on the fabric of the building and reporting to the churchwardens
- preparation of the marriage registers
- welcoming visitors.

Where a church has a sacristan or clerk, some of these duties will be their responsibility. Vergers may receive a fee for funerals and weddings but these are not fixed.

Organist

Although some churches will have a volunteer organist, most organists are paid either by an annual salary or through fees. Responsibilities can vary considerably. Some may only be required for a service once a month and for the occasional wedding or funeral; others will be full-time with responsibility not only for playing the organ but also for directing the choir, in which case there may even be an assistant organist as well.

If the organist is a paid employee, the PCC has the normal obligations of an employer and a written contract of employment is advisable. The Royal School of Church Music has model contracts. The School no longer publishes recommended rates of salary or fees except to its members and associates. It recognises that any such recommendation is only a starting point for negotiation between the organist and the incumbent and PCC because local situations vary so greatly.

In most circumstances, relations between the organist and the incumbent and PCC are positive but they can sometimes be a source of friction. Often this takes the form of a 'power struggle' and even a clash of musical taste. Organists and choirs can be quite powerful, but ultimately they are there to serve the worship of the church, not to use the church as a vehicle for their performance.

Youth worker

Work with young people is often a concern for PCCs. Some feel too daunted even to attempt it. For others it is a major aspect of their mission outreach and service. Most fall somewhere in between. Whether the youth leaders are salaried and full-time, employed on a sessional basis or volunteers, the PCC has responsibilities under safeguarding, health and safety and employment legislation. If the PCC is undertaking this for the first time, it is advisable to obtain advice from the diocesan youth officer. Youth workers should be appropriately trained.

Architect/Surveyor

Church buildings, especially the older ones, need almost constant attention and they must be inspected by a qualified architect or surveyor on a recommended list produced by the diocese every five years (the quinquennial inspection established by the Inspection of Churches Measure 1955). The inspection report indicates the work that needs to be done and usually gives this a priority-ordering together with a broad indication of the likely cost. It is a very useful document for a PCC in fulfilling its responsibility for the care of the church building.

Parishes are often recommended to use this same architect or surveyor as their professional adviser for repairs and alterations etc., as this ensures continuity and appropriate expertise. Domestic or commercial architects may be very good at their jobs but may not have the specialist knowledge which is vital when dealing with medieval buildings. The temptation is always to look for the cheapest, but experience indicates that this is usually a false economy. The right architect/surveyor will be an invaluable friend to the PCC, not only advising on necessary repairs or reordering work, but also assisting with what is sometimes felt to be the daunting task of preparing applications for faculties, including statements of need and statements of significance, and applications for grants – e.g., from the Heritage Lottery Fund.

From time to time PCCs do have reason to change their architect/surveyor, but when they do this it is vital that they settle all outstanding fees payable to the previous adviser.

Useful websites:

The Guild of Vergers
http://cofegv.org.uk/

The Royal School of Church Music
http://www.rscm.com/

Youth work
https://www.churchofengland.org/education/children-young-people/youth.aspx

http://www.childrenssociety.org.uk/what-you-can-do/your-church/worship-resources/leaps-and-bounds-good-childhood-youth-toolkit/youth-wo

Care and inspection of churches
http://www.churchcare.co.uk/churches/church-buildings-council

http://www.buildingconservation.com/

Chapter 5

Meetings

There are some people who just love meetings. The majority put up with them. Some have to go to meetings but hate them. It isn't the type of meeting that matters – it's the way they are organised and run. This is as true of PCC meetings as of any other. Clergy apart, everyone is a volunteer and they don't have to be there. Commitment, the desire to serve, a sense of duty, there was no one else willing to be elected, it gives you something to do, wanting to make a difference – the reasons for attending are numerous and varied. Whatever they are, no one enjoys a badly run meeting that seems to have no purpose, that goes on and on and on, that ends up being a wrangle or where the decisions seem to have been made beforehand. One would like to think that at PCC meetings everyone acts with respect, trust and good humour, but sadly it isn't always true. Christians can be badly organised, bitchy, bad-tempered, sulky and awkward like anyone else, but things can be done to help ensure this isn't the norm. Good management of a meeting doesn't mean there is no disagreement, no lively debate, no searching questions asked, but it does mean it shouldn't just deteriorate into personal attack or whingeing.

What follows is certainly not the last word about meetings. Volumes have been written about them and in the business world there are any amount of courses and training programmes to help meetings run smoothly and effectively. What follows are some basic guidelines and fundamental to it all is the point that, while certain people may have particular responsibilities, it is in fact the responsibility of everyone present to make a meeting go well.

Calling a meeting

As we saw in Chapter Three when considering the annual meetings, there is usually a prescribed time for giving notice of when and where a meeting will be held.

A public notice, signed by the chair of the PCC, giving date, time and place of the PCC meeting has to be displayed on or near the main church door at least ten clear days prior to the meeting. The exception to this is when there is an emergency meeting and then the chair has to give members at least three clear days' notice, in writing, indicating the purpose of the meeting. At such an emergency meeting only the business indicated on the notice may be discussed.

Not less than seven days before the meeting every member should receive in writing a notice of the meeting giving date, time and place, signed by the secretary. The notice should contain the agenda and include any resolutions or other business that have been received by the secretary. The exception to this is the meeting of the PCC that follows immediately after the APCM when the business solely involves the election of officers. The ten days' notice mentioned in the previous paragraph is still required.

Sometimes, for very good reason, a meeting has to be postponed. If the chair, the vice-chair and secretary (or any two of them) decide this is necessary, they have to give notice to all the members together with details of when the meeting will then be held. This should be within 14 days of the original date.

If at least one third of all the PCC members sign a written request for a meeting, and the PCC chair fails to convene one, they can do so themselves.

Frequency

No one likes meetings just for the sake of it when there is no real purpose and nothing of any significance to discuss.

There should be at least four meetings of the PCC a year, reasonably spread across the year. Some parishes, seeking to keep the number of meetings to a minimum, will include the meeting immediately following the APCM as one of the four.

Papers

A frequent source of complaint from members at a meeting is the lack of proper information about the business to be discussed. There are obviously times when a matter arises at the last moment or information just cannot be obtained prior to the meeting, but in the vast majority of cases there is no reason why papers should not be sent out in good time, giving members the opportunity to read and consider them. There is then no excuse for not having read them or for only doing so at the meeting itself. Such things do happen!

It is the secretary's responsibility to make sure papers go out in good time. Most important are the agenda and the minutes of the last meeting (unless previously circulated). Some papers, such as those relating to finance, the quinquennial inspection report or grant applications can be quite complex and people do need time to digest them. Whether copies of PCC correspondence received or sent are provided will depend on their complexity and what they are about. This will be a matter for the secretary's judgement and members should indicate if they do not receive what they feel they need, or if they are getting unnecessary papers.

Agenda

The agenda sets out the business of the meeting and it should be dealt with in the order given, unless the meeting resolves to do otherwise. Some PCCs find it helpful if an indication of the time likely to be given to each item is specified. It can also be helpful if a brief indication of the reason for the item is given. For example, just putting 'Church Hall' may not mean very much if it hasn't been discussed previously. It would be helpful to indicate what the item relates to – e.g., 'lettings', 'repair', 'cleaning', 'disposal'. If a resolution is to be proposed, it should be clearly set out.

Any item of business not on the agenda can only be discussed if three quarters of those present agree.

It is usual to require that notice of Any Other Business be given to the chair or secretary prior to the meeting and the notice of the meeting may well indicate this. However, there are times when something comes up at the last minute. If this is a significant matter requiring considerable discussion, it is helpful if the meeting knows at the start and not right at the very end of the meeting. To enable this, it is possible to put an item near the beginning of the agenda asking for notice of any such matter even though the discussion will not occur until Any Other Business at the end. This helps the chair manage the meeting better and to decide whether to recommend that the item be discussed or postponed to a later date.

In planning an agenda it is important that the chair/secretary has a clear idea of the purpose of the meeting and why a particular item has been included.

Quorum

The PCC cannot transact any business if there are less than one third of the members present. Decisions are made by the majority of the members present and voting. The chair of a PCC meeting has a casting vote where there is a tie.

Minutes

A clear and accurate record of the proceedings of the meeting is important. It is not sufficient for members to spare a secretary's feelings by saying about a muddled minute, 'Well, we know what she meant and in any case we all remember what we said.' People often do not remember and in any case the minutes need to be clear and unambiguous to avoid any dispute at a later date as to what was decided or said at the meeting.

While it is helpful to have some indication of the discussion and especially a record of significant, dissenting views on a matter where the vote was close, the minutes should not be a verbatim report. This is merely tedious.

The minutes should record:

- the names of members present

- if required by at least one fifth of members present, the names of those voting for and against a resolution

- if any member requires, how he/she voted on any resolution.

Minutes must be made available to all PCC members and they also have the right of access to past minutes which the chair and vice-chair deem relevant to current business. The bishop, independent examiner/auditor and archdeacon may also see minutes even without the authorisation of the PCC. Other people whose names are on the church electoral roll also have the right to see approved minutes, apart from any the PCC has resolved are confidential.

Committees

The PCC should have a Standing Committee of not less than five members, to include the minister, the churchwardens and at least two other PCC members appointed by the PCC to hold office until the next APCM. The job of the Standing Committee is to deal with the business of the PCC between meetings in line with any directions given by the PCC.

Other committees can be set up to handle the PCC's various areas of work – e.g., mission, worship, social events, fund-raising. The PCC should decide and record the composition and powers of any such committees and the minister has the right to be a member ex officio of them.

Meeting management

While the paperwork and structure of a meeting can help to make it effective, at the end of the day this will largely depend on the way the meeting is handled. The chair has a clear responsibility for this.

In most PCCs the chair will be likely to have a reasonable understanding of the members and will know who are the quiet ones, those who always ask awkward questions, the chatterboxes and the 'barrack-room lawyers'. It is important that a culture of 'respectful listening' be developed and that disagreement be dealt with in a way that does not silence dissenting voices, but equally does not allow only the loudest to be heard. Some members may find it quite difficult to speak, yet when they do so their point is helpful and wise. The chair will need to be on the look-out for this and to make sure such a person has an appropriate opportunity to make their contribution.

Most PCC meetings begin with prayer, and business should be conducted in the light of that and with an acknowledgement that what the PCC is dealing with may be 'business', but it is the business of God's church and its mission.

A chair may feel that at some point in a discussion the best way forward is to call for a pause and a time of reflection before proceeding further or taking a vote.

It is up to the chair to ensure that the business is carried out within a reasonable time and does not drag on endlessly. Two hours should be sufficient for most normal meetings. Undue time should not be spent on procedural matters and there may well be occasions when the chair has to call discussion to an end, not least when it seems to be going round in circles.

When and whether to call for a vote is a matter of judgement. Some Christian groups – for instance, the Quakers – resolve business without ever having a vote. Chairs may seek a consensus without the formality of a vote, although members always have the right to call for one. When a vote is taken it should be clear to everyone exactly what is being voted on and afterwards what the outcome is. The chair will wish to ensure that the secretary has both the resolution and outcome clear for the minutes. Outcomes mean not only the decision and the action involved, but who will implement the decision. This too should be noted in the minutes.

While the business of a PCC is important and sometimes serious, a light touch and a sense of humour go a long way to make a meeting enjoyable as well as effective. In this, as in other ways, all the members present have a responsibility, not just the chair.

It is also important that there is a sensible and sensitive attitude about what was discussed at the meeting and what can be said outside the meeting. Some matters may be designated as confidential and this needs to be fully respected. The PCC, it should be remembered, is a corporate body and its decisions should be upheld even by those who have not agreed with them. It is all too easy for the position of a PCC or of its chair to be undermined by those who 'gossip' their opposition outside the meeting. This does not mean that a different point of view cannot be expressed, but that retelling the detail of the PCC discussion is inappropriate, especially if it includes personal comments about members. If this is felt to be too fierce a restraint, then a person may need to give serious thought about whether or not they can appropriately continue as a PCC member.

Chapter Six

Teams, Groups and Plurality

By and large this brief guide has been based on the situation of a PCC in a single parish benefice or where parishes in a benefice have not been formed into a team. There are special provisions to cover teams, groups and where benefices are held in plurality (they share the same incumbent). It is important that advice be sought if there is uncertainty about what should happen in these circumstances. Much of the legal position is contained in the Church Representation Rules, but other legislation is also relevant.

What follows are some of the more basic points.

Teams and groups are set up by Pastoral Schemes. Where this has been done, the parishes in the team or group may, at their APCMs, pass a resolution to establish a joint scheme in order to set up a team council or a group council.

Team councils

The members of a **team council** are:

- the team rector

- other members of the ministry team

- every assistant curate, deaconess and lay worker licensed to a parish in the team who are not members of the ministry team

- lay representatives from each of the PCCs within the team. The number of these representatives, and the manner in which they are chosen or appointed are set out in the scheme setting up the team council.

The scheme also provides for matters such as who chairs the team council, its meetings and procedures. Depending on the provisions of the scheme, and with some specific exceptions, a PCC in the team may delegate to the team council certain of its functions as it thinks fit.

All members of the ministry team are entitled to attend and take part in the proceedings of the APCMs of all the parishes in the team.

Group councils

The members of a **group council** are:

- all the members of the group ministry

- every assistant curate, deaconess and lay worker licensed to a parish in the group

- lay representatives from each of the PCCs within the group. The number of these representatives, and the manner in which they are chosen or appointed are set out in the scheme setting up the group council.

The comments above about other matters and delegation by PCCs in the case of team councils also apply to group councils.

All incumbents and priests in charge of parishes within the group are entitled to attend and take part in the APCMs of all the parishes in the group. They are also entitled to attend the PCC meetings of each of the parishes in the group and to receive papers circulated to PCC members. They may speak at the meetings but not vote.

Plurality and Joint councils

Parishes in a multi-parish benefice that is not a team or in benefices held in plurality (under the same incumbent) may at the APCM make a joint scheme to establish a joint council.

The members of a **joint council** are:

- the ministers of the parishes

- lay representatives from each of the PCCs. The number of these representatives, and the manner in which they are chosen or appointed are set out in the scheme setting up the joint council.

The scheme also provides for matters such as who chairs the joint council, its meetings and procedures. PCCs may delegate certain functions to it.

In a parish where there are **two or more places of worship** the APCM may make a scheme that ensures that the PCC has lay representatives from each of the places of worship. The APCM may also make a scheme for a district council for such a place of worship, indicating its membership and powers. Among other exceptions, these delegated powers may not include the production of separate financial statements.

The advice of the diocesan registrar should be sought in setting up any of these schemes.

Postword

Judy,

Thanks for the book. There was quite a bit to take in. I hadn't realised there was so much to it and I can see it's a serious responsibility being on the PCC. I'm not sure I shall be able to contribute much to some of the discussions, but certainly I could help with the buildings side of things. So, nothing daunted, I'd be happy to stand for the PCC (if people will nominate and second me!). With a reasonable amount of notice I should be able to get to meetings.

As ever
Geoff